D1524709

Teen Guide to
FANDOMS
Gaming, Music, Movies, and More

Stuart A. Kallen

HALF HOLLOW HILLS
COMMUNITY LIBRARY
55 VANDERBILT PKWY
DIX HILLS, NY 11746

ReferencePoint
Press®

San Diego, CA

About the Author

Stuart A. Kallen is the author of more than 350 nonfiction books for children and young adults. He has written on topics ranging from the theory of relativity to the art of electronic dance music. In 2018 Kallen won a Green Earth Book Award from the Nature Generation environmental organization for his book *Trashing the Planet: Examining the Global Garbage Glut*. In his spare time, he is a singer, songwriter, and guitarist in San Diego.

© 2024 ReferencePoint Press, Inc.
Printed in the United States

For more information, contact:
ReferencePoint Press, Inc.
PO Box 27779
San Diego, CA 92198
www.ReferencePointPress.com

ALL RIGHTS RESERVED.
No part of this work covered by the copyright hereon may be reproduced or used in any form or by any means—graphic, electronic, or mechanical, including photocopying, recording, taping, web distribution, or information storage retrieval systems—without the written permission of the publisher.

Picture Credits:
Cover: Shutterstock.com

5: Fred Duval/Shutterstock.com
8: Richard Levine/Alamy Stock Photo
11: CJG - Technology/Alamy Stock Photo
14: OFA/ZOJ/Oscar Gonzalez/WENN/Newscom
18: ZUMA Press, Inc./Alamy Stock Photo
20: NurPhoto SRL/Alamy Stock Photo
25: DFree/Shutterstock.com

28: Sipa USA/Alamy Stock Photo
32: PA Images/Alamy Stock Photo
35: Myriam B/iStock
38: Unwind/Shutterstock.com
41: Imageplotter/Alamy Stock Photo
44: Photofest Images
48: The Dark Knight/Shutterstock.com
52: Visions of America, LLC/Alamy Stock Photo
54: dpa picture alliance/Alamy Stock Photo

LIBRARY OF CONGRESS CATALOGING-IN-PUBLICATION DATA

Names: Kallen, Stuart A., 1955- author.
Title: Teen guide to fandoms : gaming, music, movies, and more / by Stuart A. Kallen.
Description: San Diego, CA : ReferencePoint Press, Inc., 2024. | Includes bibliographical references and index.
Identifiers: LCCN 2023018247 (print) | LCCN 2023018248 (ebook) | ISBN 9781678206109 (library binding) | ISBN 9781678206116 (ebook)
Subjects: LCSH: Subculture--Juvenile literature. | Fans (Persons)--Juvenile literature. | Mass media--Social aspects--Juvenile literature.
Classification: LCC HM646 .K358 2022 (print) | LCC HM646 (ebook) | DDC 305.23--dc23/eng/20230502
LC record available at https://lccn.loc.gov/2023018247
LC ebook record available at https://lccn.loc.gov/2023018248

CONTENTS

Fandom and Fan Culture

Almost everyone is a fan of something. Most people have a favorite movie, television series, band, book, team, or video game. But fan culture, or fandom, goes beyond downloading a beloved band's newest album or streaming the latest episode of a popular show. Superfans are not just consumers; they are participants in a fan culture that can include millions of other people with similar tastes and beliefs. And some fans are so committed that they use their fandom as a creative outlet to produce fan fiction, art, videos, comics, costumes, and songs to honor their idols.

Fandom is a feeling of camaraderie with others who share the same interests. Those who are fans of a band, anime, film, or team feel a sense of belonging. They connect with others who share that passion and want to express their dedication. Mental health therapist Meredith Hrebenak (a self-described fangirl of the television show *Supernatural)* believes fandom can be a healthy form of self-expression. According to Hrebenak, when fans see their own issues reflected in fictional characters, they develop a deeper understanding of themselves and empathy for others who are equally obsessed:

> There are unique opportunities for self-expression within fandom life. For some people, who may not identify with typical "social norms," fandom provides a safe place where "weirdness" is not only welcomed but celebrated. Self-expression can relate to thoughts, feelings, values, religion, politics, personality, etc. and can allow people to be authentic and enhance relationships.[1]

Geeks and Stans

There is little doubt that the internet propelled fandom into the mainstream during the twenty-first century. Originally known as geek culture, the massive popularity of pop music acts such as Taylor Swift, One Direction, and BTS changed the widespread perception of fandom during the 2010s. What was once viewed as a mass of screaming teenage girls evolved into a positive image of fans who participate in a culture by providing their own creative input. Along the way, the objects of fan adoration have been promoted as cultural ambassadors and have become topics for scholarly research. In 2018 the Korean pop group BTS addressed the United Nations General Assembly. Swift's lyrics and impact on the culture are subjects for study at the University of Texas, New York University, and other learning institutions. Dedicated fans who are scientists have even applied the names

of their favorite artists to their discoveries. Australian entomologist (insect researcher) Bryan Lessard named a horsefly after his favorite singer, Beyoncé. The previously unnamed insect with a golden abdomen and honey-colored wings is now known as *Scaptia beyonceae*. Lessard says he hopes the horsefly will be "an ambassador for bootylicious biodiversity."[2] There are also bugs named after Taylor Swift, Andrew Garfield, and Shakira. A genus of fern bearing Lady Gaga's name includes a nod to her

Lady Gaga is pictured in 2022 at the British Film Academy Awards in London. Stars like Lady Gaga earn billions of dollars from superfans who spend money on downloads, clothing, accessories, toys, games, and concert tickets.

fans; *Gaga monstraparva* refers to Gaga's superfans, whom she calls "Little Monsters."

Fandom is not always exhibited in such positive ways. Some fans become so obsessive that they fall behind in school and become socially isolated. And in a digital world populated by trolls, cyberbullies, and celebrity takedowns, it is no surprise that rival fans often engage in battles and beefs.

The loudest and most committed superfans proudly call themselves "stans"; the term was taken from an Eminem song, "Stan," about a superfan who becomes a dangerous stalker. The die-hard fans trade barbs on what is known as Stan Twitter and in similar groups on TikTok, Tumblr, and elsewhere. Culture reporter Joe Coscarelli writes, "These devotees . . . pledge allegiance to their favorites like the most rabid political partisans or religious followers. They organize to win awards show polls, boost sales and raise money like grass roots activists. And they band together to pester—or harass, and even dox—those who may dare to slight the stars they have chosen to align themselves with."[3]

The entertainment industry has no problem with stan culture. Idols earn billions of dollars from superfans who spend money on downloads, clothing, accessories, toys, games, and concert tickets. Lady Gaga superfan Benjamin Cordero explains, "You might have a [casual fan] buy a record. But a person on Stan Twitter probably bought that record 10 times, streamed a song on three separate playlists and racked up hundreds and hundreds of plays. It's basically promotion, free labor [for the artist]."[4]

Although there are some negative aspects to fan culture, fandom continues to provide a sense of community and purpose to participants. Fans make lifelong friends they never would have discovered otherwise. And the excitement and sense of purpose associated with fandom can help ease life's little disappointments, boost a person's outlook, and provide insights that last a lifetime.

CHAPTER ONE

The Growth of Online Fan Culture

Graphic artist Emily Kelley is a Swiftie, a superfan of singer-songwriter Taylor Swift. Kelley creates artwork based on Swift's songs. In 2022 she created an illustration of silhouettes dancing in the moonlight inspired by Swift's hit song "All Too Well." Kelley uploaded an illustration video to TikTok that struck a chord with Swifties. One fan commented, "Why are there tears in my eyes watching this?"[5] Kelley, who was working to create an illustration for every song in Swift's discography, had more than 135,000 followers on TikTok in 2023. She was able to combine her talent with her fandom to create a business selling Swift-related merchandise.

Kelley is one of countless fans who use online platforms to sell celebrity-inspired artwork, jewelry, clothing, and other merchandise. According to Kelley, "Fans know what [other] fans want. I'm listening to every single song, watching every interview, and picking apart every social media post from my favorite artists. I think that reflects in the products I create."[6]

Early Internet Fandom

Kelley's statement exemplifies the central role of the internet in modern fan culture. She can listen to every song, watch videos of interviews and concerts, find out the latest news, and carry on personal conversations with other fans without leaving her room.

There is little doubt that those who consider themselves Swifties, Little Monsters, Harry Styles's Stylers, or members of other fan groups are innovators when it comes to using the internet to

There is a huge demand for celebrity-inspired merchandise. This photo shows Taylor Swift merchandise at a pop-up shop in New York City in 2019.

promote their favorite acts. But the concept of superfans collecting every song, creating fan artwork, selling homemade T-shirts, and bonding with one another goes back to earlier times. During the 1960s, for example, pop artists had legions of fans who collected magazines, posters, toys, and records and then formed fan clubs to discuss their passions. The Beatles—perhaps the preeminent group to inspire such widespread worship—had millions of dedicated fans around the world.

Another group founded in the 1960s, the Grateful Dead, attracted fans who developed a distinct culture based on the band's music and concert performances. Emerging out of the psychedelic hippy scene in the San Francisco Bay Area during the 1960s, the Grateful Dead seemed to personify the laid-back, antiestablishment ethos of the counterculture. The band's ardent fans—known as Deadheads—embraced this attitude, but that did not mean they were out of touch with innovation. Some of the original Deadheads were computer scientists who attended Stanford University in Palo Alto, California. One of them, Paul Martin, saw a new way to stay in touch with his Deadhead friends via early computer networks. In 1973 Martin used the supercomputers at the Stanford Artificial Intelligence Laboratory (SAIL) to collect and distribute Deadhead emails.

In early 1975, Martin made the Grateful Dead mailing list semi-public by putting it on ARPANET, an early version of the internet. According to culture reporter and One Direction superfan Kaitlyn Tiffany, "Martin programmed automatic news updates that crawled for information about the Grateful Dead and sent them out immediately to all subscribers, and they, in turn, crowdsourced information from other fans in a manner and with a purpose strikingly similar to the pop stans of today."[7]

New Tech Attracts Fans

Deadheads created hundreds of dial-up bulletin boards during the 1980s. These forums, which connected computers through telephone lines, allowed users to post simple messages. They were widely used before the World Wide Web was created in 1994. The subjects covered on early bulletin boards would be familiar to any twenty-first-century superfan. Deadheads analyzed lyrics, shared concert setlists, and arranged meetups. Before the advent of music streaming, audience members who recorded Grateful Dead concerts found one another on bulletin boards and arranged to share cassette tapes through snail mail.

The most popular bulletin board was a Bay Area virtual community known as the WELL, short for Whole Earth 'Lectronic Link. Users were charged by the minute on its dial-up service. Although the WELL was initially used by scientists and academics, membership swelled after it was discovered by Deadheads. This helped ensure the service's survival, according to the WELL's first director, Matthew McClure: "Suddenly, we had an onslaught of new users. The Deadheads came online and seemed to know instinctively how to use the system to create a community around themselves. . . . [The WELL was] so phenomenally successful that for the first several years, Deadheads were by far the single largest source of income for the enterprise."[8]

By the mid-1990s, the World Wide Web was growing in popularity, and superfans were responsible for creating some of the most heavily trafficked web pages. Television shows such as *The X-Files* and *Buffy the Vampire Slayer*, along with the early anime series *Sailor Moon*, had their own fan sites. Pages for musical acts such as NSYNC, Britney Spears, and the Backstreet Boys also expanded as fans added thousands of photos and other data.

Pop superstar David Bowie was a leading innovator in creating a home for fans online. In 1998 Bowie launched the first artist-based internet service provider (ISP) called BowieNet. Fans paid around twenty dollars a month for access to Bowie chat rooms, exclusive musical content, and a davidbowie.com email address. As Bowie said at the time, the ISP was "a single place where the vast archives of music information could be accessed, views stated and ideas exchanged."[9] Bowie's site ran for eight years.

Pottermania

Bowie launched his ISP at a time when the online world was expanding at an incredible rate. Between 1997 and 2000, the number of Americans using the internet more than quadrupled from 70 million to more than 300 million, according to the Internet World Stats website. This three-year period coincided with the release of the first four books in the blockbuster Harry Potter series by J.K. Rowling.

The internet proved to be a magical tool for the growing legion of fans called Potterheads. Harry Potter fan Melissa Anelli says, "The Internet changed Harry Potter about as much as the Internet was changing everything else."[10] Emerson Spartz started one of the biggest fan sites, MuggleNet, in 1999 when he was twelve years old. Within a year, the site was attracting hundreds of thousands of daily visitors who could read fan fiction and participate in discussion forums and role-playing games. MuggleNet even

A girl looks at the Harry Potter Facebook fan page. There are many different websites dedicated to the Harry Potter series, and these sites have helped the series become even more popular.

provided fans with dozens of recipes based on foods mentioned in the Harry Potter books. On the date Rowling published the fifth title, *Order of the Phoenix*, in 2003, MuggleNet hosted a release party at an Illinois shopping mall that attracted more than ten thousand Potterheads. A similar event was held two years later when book six, *Half-Blood Prince*, was released. By that time, Harry Potter book release events were staged in cities throughout North America and Europe.

MuggleNet, which remains active today, was only one of hundreds of fan sites dedicated to Pottermania. As eleven-year-old Potterhead Rachel Ruskin said in 2002, "There are, like, millions of Web sites."[11] One of those sites, the Leaky Cauldron, was a forum where Potterheads dissected stories for hidden clues about character motives and discussed news about upcoming books and films. Dozens of sites were dedicated to Potter fan fiction, which featured fan-created stories that could run up to several hundred pages in length. Heidi Tandy, who founded a fan fiction site called FictionAlley in 2001, was even contacted by Warner

Real-Life Quidditch

Perhaps nothing better exemplifies how Harry Potter fans have come together to transform the world than the founding of the US Quidditch Association in 2007. Author J.K. Rowling first described the sport of quidditch in the 1997 book *Harry Potter and the Philosopher's Stone*. The sport was played by witches and wizards who chased a leather ball, called a quaffle, while flying on broomsticks.

In 2005, students at Middlebury College in Vermont invented a real-life version of quidditch. Players try to score goals by chasing five quaffles around on a grass field like the one described by Rowling. They must keep a broomstick between their legs during play. As news of the quidditch team spread online, the sport was picked up by Potter fans throughout the world. The International Quidditch Association (IQA) was formed in 2009 as a governing body for the sport. According to the IQA, in 2023, thousands of people were competing in quidditch leagues in more than forty countries.

Bros., the studio that produced the Harry Potter films. While other publishers and film producers were forcing fan sites to shut down because they were using material that was copyrighted, Warner Bros. gave FictionAlley its official blessing by displaying a link on its official Harry Potter website.

Rowling has said in interviews that she was flattered by the proliferation of grassroots fan sites. She even began handing out awards for fan sites. In 2004 the first site to receive the honor was called Immeritus, which was devoted to the character Sirius Black. Rowling wrote on her official website that she loved the fact that a somewhat minor character had gained a passionate fan club.

The love that Harry Potter fans showed for their favorite books helped boost the entire young adult (YA) publishing market during the late 2000s. Fans of the Twilight and Hunger Games series followed the trail blazed by Potterheads, while single books such as *The Fault in Our Stars* also attracted legions of fans who created their own art, fan fiction, costumes, and related paraphernalia. Journalist Laura Miller writes, "While I was researching a

2012 piece about the publication of Suzanne Collins' *The Hunger Games*, sources told me again and again that online networks of YA bloggers, vloggers, and social media mavens had played a major role in the book's success, and that most of these 'influencers,' all women in their 20s, had roots in *Potter* fandom."[12]

Moving in One Direction

As YA readers were pushing book sales higher, similar dynamics were shaking up the music industry. By the early 2010s, technological advances, including faster computers, the growth of high-speed internet systems, and wireless communications, were fueling a social media explosion. And websites such as Facebook, YouTube, Twitter, and Tumblr were relatively new tools being used to supercharge online fandom. One of the groups at the center of this new digital landscape was the British boy band One Direction. Tech journalist Nilay Patel wrote in 2022, "One Direction created much of the online culture we live in today on social platforms."[13]

One Direction did not have glamorous beginnings. The group was made up of five British teens who auditioned for *The X-Factor*, the British version of *American Idol*, in 2010. Individually, the singers did not impress show creator Simon Cowell, but he thought he could put them together to make a good boy band. He said he made the decision in about ten minutes.

> "One Direction created much of the online culture we live in today on social platforms."[13]
>
> —Nilay Patel, tech journalist

One Direction famously lost *The X-Factor* after appearing in several episodes. Despite placing third in the competition, the group impressed hundreds of mostly female British fans, who found one another online. What followed was a social media frenzy that was unique at the time. "[One Direction] had this grassroots fandom that really dedicated itself to what you could call media manipulation, tweeting constantly in highly interconnected groups and figuring out how to use these platforms to make something they cared about super visible,"[14] Tiffany explains.

"200 or 300 super-fans made it their job to promote [One Direction] around the world . . . [and I] saw something I've never seen before in the music business, which is fans, not a record label, marketing and promoting a band worldwide."[15]

—Simon Cowell, entertainment executive

Within two years, propelled by their online fandom, One Direction became the best-selling musical act on Earth. It was the first band in history to have its first four albums debut at number one on the *Billboard* charts, and One Direction's stadium concerts sold out in minutes. But Cowell says he does not deserve credit for the band's success:

> 200 or 300 super-fans made it their job to promote this band around the world . . . [and I] saw something I've never seen before in the music business, which is fans, not a record label, marketing and promoting a band worldwide. From the second [*The X-Factor*] finished, the fans made it their mission that One Direction were going to become the biggest band in the world.[15]

This photo shows (from left to right) One Direction members Niall Horan, Zayn Malik, Liam Payne, Harry Styles, and Louis Tomlinson at a 2015 awards show in Madrid, Spain.

Fandom Can Be Good for Mental Health

Being part of a fan group can be a lot of fun. Fandom allows people to make new friends and share interests while providing an outlet for creative expression. These positive aspects of fandom would be impossible without social media. It provides a place for fans to post their fan fiction and artwork or just stay up-to-date on the latest news about their favorite source of entertainment.

Psychologists say fandom can also be good for mental health. Psychotherapist and psychology professor Laurel Steinberg comments on this:

> Belonging to a fandom group helps [fans] connect to other like-minded youths on social media throughout the year, as well as at concert events. . . . Connecting with people over shared passions and interests is good for mental and emotional health because it helps to create a fraternity-like or family-like sense of security. It's also generally fun to scheme and get excited about something with others, and gives them a subject to talk about that they know will always be well received.

These mental health benefits can counter feelings of loneliness that can lead to depression. And fandom helps people of diverse backgrounds find community in a culture that is often marked by division and conflict.

Quoted in Brianna Wiest, "Psychologists Say that Belonging to Fandom Is Amazing for Your Mental Health," *Teen Vogue* July 20, 2017. www.teenvogue.com.

One Direction returned the favor by producing a flood of social media content for fans, known as Directioners. Beginning in 2010, band members uploaded weekly clips to the One Direction Video Diary channel on YouTube. The videos provided fans with glimpses into their daily lives, from hanging around backstage to eating meals together. Online content creator and self-proclaimed superfan Amy Astrid explains the importance of the videos: "The comments [on those video diaries] were a place for people to share their thoughts. It made their growing audience feel like they really knew the boys."[16]

The band's fame continued to grow, and fan communities thrived on social media platforms such as Twitter; Astrid says the

One Direction Twitter thread attracted more than 160,000 followers. "Whenever they were on tour, there were new things to talk about every day, so that encouraged fans to spend a lot of time on Twitter engaging with other fan accounts,"[17] she states.

Fandom Goes Mainstream

In 2019 journalist Aja Romano wrote, "At the start of this decade, 'fandom' wasn't a word most people knew, much less fully understood. . . . It's been known mainly to people who considered themselves to be in fandom."[18] By the end of the 2010s, however, the online culture developed by book lovers and top-selling music acts was adopted by others. Fans of anime, video games, movies, and television shows all used social media and video streaming services to promote their idols and pan their rivals. Looking back on Pottermania, Miller writes,

> Fandom itself has gone from being about a passion for a particular story or set of characters to a kind of self-sustaining identity. . . . Fannishness about Rowling's books has morphed into fannishness in general, and even fannishness about fannishness itself. Instead of the preoccupation of a rather secretive, sheepish minority of people mocked for their geeky passions, fandom had become a badge of honor, even a claim to fame. It feels like home to vast numbers of people who grew up in the 2000s.[19]

CHAPTER TWO

Pop Idols: Music Fandom

Beachwood Canyon is a fashionable community in the Hollywood Hills area of Los Angeles that has long been home to movie stars and other celebrities. But most visitors lining up outside the Beachwood Cafe in early 2023 had only one superstar in mind—Harry Styles. The restaurant patrons refer to themselves as Harrys, Harries, or Stylers. They have been crowding into the mom-and-pop restaurant since 2019, when Styles used its name in the song "Falling" from the album *Fine Line*. Stylers believe the moody ballad is about the model and actress Camille Rowe, a former Beachwood Canyon resident, who dated Styles from 2017 to 2018.

Styles rose to fame as a singer in One Direction. A year after the band took an indefinite break in 2016, Styles released his first solo album, *Harry Styles*. It debuted at number one on the *Billboard* 200 charts and went on to become one of the top-selling albums worldwide in 2017. Styles continued to top the charts and break sales records with *Fine Line* and the 2022 album *Harry's House*.

On the Saturday that Styles played the Kia Forum in Los Angeles in 2023, the number of Stylers showing up for coffee at the Beachwood Cafe had increased dramatically. Wait times for tables stretched to more than three hours. Colorfully dressed fans from across the country packed into the booths and ordered the Beachwood Scramble, an egg dish Styles once ate at the restaurant. Someone started singing "Falling," and almost everyone

Fans crowd around Harry Styles at a 2022 performance in New York City. Styles rose to fame with the band One Direction, and then went solo in 2017. More than six thousand fans attended this 2022 performance.

in the cafe joined in. Some brought cardboard cutouts of Styles for photos, and some of the cafe staff kept track of the action by monitoring TikTok and Instagram. One of the Stylers in the crowd, twenty-six-year-old Noelle Jay, was extremely excited about visiting the cafe where Styles once ate breakfast: "It's panic-inducing; I could literally evaporate thinking about it. . . . He's like my comfort person, my light, my inspiration, all of the above."[20]

Bieber Beliebers

Harry Styles and Justin Bieber were both born in 1994, and they both started their careers as teen singing sensations. There has been a rivalry between the two singers—and their fans—going back to the days of One Direction. The fan conflict came to a head in 2014 when MTV presented the Europe Music Awards. The show's producers asked fans to vote for their favorite act on social media using hashtags for each nominee. The act with the most hashtags would win the MTV Biggest Fans Award.

The contest set off a massive Twitter marathon between Directioners and Bieber fans, called Beliebers. The race quickly became the trending subject on Twitter worldwide as the acts locked into a dead heat, each attracting 89 million votes. By comparison, third-place Ariana Grande only received 5 million votes.

Both sides in the epic Twitter war engaged in dirty tricks. Fans created fake hashtags hoping they would be picked up by their rivals. The hashtags were deliberately sabotaged, containing emojis that would disqualify them from being counted. In the end, One Direction won the Biggest Fans Award along with Best Pop Award and Best Live Act Award. Bieber won the MTV Europe Music Award for best male performer.

While Beliebers and Directioners were in a head-to-head competition during the mid-2010s, Bieber already had a unique claim to fame: he was one of the first teen idols created by the internet. Bieber was only twelve when he began posting performance videos on YouTube in 2009. A video of a rhythm and blues song of his was accidentally discovered by American talent scout Scott "Scooter" Braun, who was searching for a different artist at the time. Braun was impressed enough to sign Bieber to a recording contract. When Bieber's first single, "One Time," was released in May 2009, he became the biggest solo teen pop act since Michael Jackson rose to fame during the 1970s. By January 2010, the video of "One Time" had been viewed on YouTube more than 100 million times. By 2012, Bieber had earned over $108 million, and he said he owed much of his success to social media: "Without the internet and without YouTube, I wouldn't have gotten the chance to put my music out there and have people hear it."[21]

Bieber quickly found that the internet could be used for more than getting his music out there. He understood that he could boost his income by using social media to keep Beliebers engaged in his personal life. Bieber created a steady stream of content for social media sites that included photos of his latest tattoos and texts about his next projects. Fans returned the favor by producing an endless stream of Bieber artwork; some of the fan art was later used on his 2015 album, *Purpose*.

Bieber succeeded in keeping his fans talking about him by feeding controversies about his love life, including his relationship with ex-girlfriend Selena Gomez. Although it was public knowledge that Bieber had broken up with Gomez, he continued to post photos of the two together without explanation. This caused a spike in Twitter threads by Beliebers debating the actual relationship status of the couple. Bieber kept the fans tweeting by sharing intimate photos of himself with other women. Each picture set off a social media explosion when influencers such as Kendall Jenner and Kourtney Kardashian began talking about Bieber. This, in turn, got Bieber's name mentioned in newspapers, magazines, television entertainment shows, and elsewhere in mainstream media. Meanwhile, Bieber never commented on the rumors. Entertainment blogger Luca Macera writes, "This form of social media management is unique to the industry. Where most celebrities feel the need to carefully address stories of themselves in the public in order to keep their reputation safe, Justin Bieber couldn't care less. He posted both content that pleased his fans and pleased the media by giving them stories to write about."[22]

Justin Bieber is pictured in 2020 at the Los Angeles premiere of a YouTube show about his life. Bieber has actively used social media and the internet to keep fans engaged in his personal life.

Taylor Swift Breaks the Internet

Taylor Swift is another superstar who began her career as a teen. Swift was only sixteen when she released her first single, "Tim McGraw," in 2005, which launched her career as a country music sensation. When Swift released *Fearless* in November 2008, the album had the largest opening for any female artist in any musical category that year. Five singles from *Fearless* entered the top ten on both country and pop charts.

Swift went on to become a cultural icon who continues to expertly use social media to keep her fans engaged. In 2023 Swift had a combined following of more than half a billion followers on social media platforms. The superstar singer treats Swifties to picture-perfect portraits, clips of backstage antics, adorable photos of her cat, and concert clips. She also informs her fans about her upcoming tours, record releases, and television appearances. But Swift does more than talk about herself on social media. She understands that her audience grew up as part of an online sharing culture. She often shares posts by unknown musicians who play her songs. These are shared and retweeted thousands of times, and Swift sometimes adds comments and encouragement. Social media marketing expert Donna Wells explains, "With every interaction, [Swift] delivers what her fans specifically love about her: humor, intelligence, accessibility and gratitude."[23]

"With every interaction, [Taylor Swift] delivers what her fans specifically love about her: humor, intelligence, accessibility and gratitude."[23]

—Donna Wells, social media marketing expert

Nothing better demonstrates the power of Swift's online fandom then the sentence written in 2021 by CNN reporter Chloe Melas: "Taylor Swift officially broke the internet on Friday."[24] Melas was referring to the release of the ten-minute video of Swift's song "All Too Well: The Short Film." Swift originally wrote the song "All Too Well" in 2011 and released it on the album *Red*. Although Swift never confirmed or denied fan speculation, the words to the song obviously refer to the singer's three-month love affair with

The Styles of Stylers

With his feather boas, sequin jumpsuits, velvet jackets, and hot pink pants, Harry Styles has been called one of the world's best-dressed male singing sensations. And when his fans, called Stylers, attend his concerts, many in the crowd are decked out in their own flamboyant outfits inspired by the superstar. In 2022 Styles's Love On Tour concert series inspired the hashtag #HSLOTOutfit, which Stylers used to share their fashion ideas. The fashion frenzy hashtag continued to attract interest after the tour ended, reaching over 500 million views on TikTok by 2023.

Some Stylers make their own clothes, spending endless hours shaping Lycra, rhinestones, and fake fur into eye-popping outfits. Bella Troy-Williamson, a twenty-three-year-old Styler, went viral on TikTok showing off her hand-crocheted sunflower dress, inspired by Styles's song "Sunflower." Twenty-one-year-old Meshaa Isaac, who became a Styler at age nine, says sharing outfit ideas helped her find a new community: "You often see the same people [on TikTok] and you start interacting with them. When they're also fans, you end up forming connections with them and even becoming friends. . . . Everyone that goes to a Harry Styles concert will agree that it's a safe space and a judgment-free zone. . . . It's just fun."

Quoted in Jumi Akinfenwa, "How Harry Styles Fans Are Redefining Concert Fashion," Refinery 29, July 7, 2022. www.refinery29.com.

actor Jake Gyllenhaal. The relationship ended when Gyllenhaal failed to show up for Swift's twenty-first birthday party in 2010. Swift rerecorded the song in 2021 along with the entire *Red* album, which she renamed *Red (Taylor's Version)*.

"All Too Well: A Short Film" features two actors with striking physical similarities to Swift and Gyllenhaal. The video accumulated over 13 million views within twenty-four hours of its debut. Swifties lit up Twitter and TikTok expressing their sympathy for Swift while condemning Gyllenhaal. Swift had been dating another man since 2016, but the song and video about a ten-year-old relationship attracted massive attention to her new release. *Red (Taylor's Version)* was streamed nearly 123 million times during its first twenty-four hours, making the release the most streamed album by a female artist in a single day.

Ticketmaster Meltdown

Swifties broke the internet again in 2022 after Swift announced she would be performing a series of concerts known as the Eras Tour. The demand for tickets was so overwhelming that the Ticketmaster website crashed, forcing the ticket vendor to stop selling tickets. Ticketmaster was prepared to sell 1.5 million tickets to fans who preregistered; however, its website could not deal with the 14 million Taylor Swift concert ticket requests it received that day. According to Greg Maffel, chief executive officer (CEO) of Ticketmaster's parent company, Live Nation, "We could've filled 900 stadiums."[25]

The Ticketmaster meltdown made headlines, as music reporters Eli Motycka and Hannah Herner only half-jokingly wrote: "We'll all remember where we were when the Ticketmaster queue was paused."[26] Swifties were devastated, and they were quick to demonstrate their collective power. A month after the debacle, twenty-six Swifties filed a class-action lawsuit against Ticketmaster, accusing the company of fraud, price fixing, and other violations. Around two hundred more joined the lawsuit after they found out about it on TikTok. Clay Murray, one of the Swifties involved in the lawsuit, explained why he got involved, saying he waited for tickets for hours only to end up "sobbing, crying, really upset." He added, "People can't afford to spend so much money, and I had done everything that I was supposed to do. It was personally devastating, and then the anger continued to grow."[27]

Ticketmaster apologized to Swift's fans, but the damage was done. Numerous Swifties complained to their elected congressional representatives, and several politicians, including New York representative Alexandria Ocasio-Cortez and Minnesota senator Amy Klobuchar got involved. They promised to write legislation that would break up Ticketmaster, which they claim holds a monopoly on ticket sales. Several months after the Ticketmaster mess, Swifties continued to get their revenge. Several company executives were required to appear at a Senate Judiciary Committee hearing

Billie Eilish Superfans Face the Elements

The weather was windy, wet, and cold in Los Angeles in early December 2022; however, that did not stop Billie Eilish superfans from braving the elements to score good general admission seats for Eilish's three-night concert at the Kia Forum. Although the first show was scheduled for December 12, fans began pitching their tents around the forum on November 30. By the time a two-day rainstorm began on December 10, around two hundred fans were in line. Eilish fan Sarah Vazquez had been camping for five days when the rain began falling: "Last night, oh my gosh it was brutal, we woke up with water in our tent and our blankets were completely soaked. In the morning I woke up and I forgot what I was even here for, but then I'm like 'I'm here for Billie, I will do anything for her.'"

Some of these die-hard fans had traveled from as far away as Germany to see their favorite singer. New Jersey resident Ryan Manning explained why she was camping at the Forum: "I had a really rough time growing up and having someone as an artist that literally went through the same experiences that I went through helped a lot."

Quoted in Clara Harter, "Through Wind and Rain, Billie Elilish Superfans Camp Outside Forum, Hope for Best Seats," *Los Angeles Daily News*, December 12, 2022. www.dailynews.com.

to answer for the problem. The hearing included Senator Richard Blumenthal quoting lyrics from Swift's song "Anti-Hero," saying that the executives should look in the mirror and admit "I'm the problem. It's me."[28]

The BTS Army

When the South Korean K-pop group BTS released its first single, "No More Dream," in 2013, the band was ready with a social media plan meant to attract loyal fans. The seven band members— V, J-Hope, RM, Jin, Jimin, Jungkook, and Suga—personally recorded video diaries, posted dance practices, took part in post-concert chats, and answered fan questions on Twitter. The personalized posting helped BTS create one of the most dedicated K-pop fan groups in the world. The so-called BTS Army (stylized as *A.R.M.Y.*, an acronym for "Adorable Representative M.C. for Youth") is made up of millions of fans. The American version of the

BTS Army is described by *Vulture* senior writer E. Alex Jung as "of every demographic, but mostly young women—Asian, black, Latina, Arab, Native American, white, and every ethnic category those words could possibly [cover]."[29]

Army members act as social media ambassadors for BTS. They make video compilations of individual band members and provide translations in several languages when the band appears on Korean television music shows. BTS followers also spend countless hours analyzing lyrics, discussing song themes, and picking apart supposedly hidden messages in photos and videos. When the album *Love Yourself: Tear* was released in 2018, one Army fan tweeted about her emotional reaction to the song "Fake Love": "It's almost 3hrs and I can't stop crying. The theory behind FAKE LOVE is haunting me. FAKE LOVE is when you love something/someone truly & madly & when you realize that everything was fake it [hurts] you forever."[30]

In 2022 BTS launched a groundbreaking new app meant to reach listeners and cultivate fans throughout the world. The social media and content app called Weverse provides fans who pay for a monthly subscription with exclusive content, including live streams of performances, promotional events, and showcases.

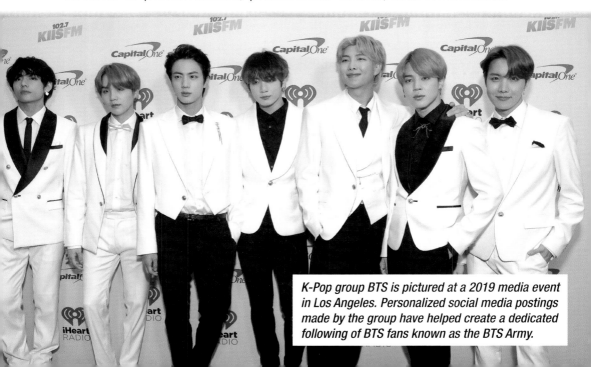

K-Pop group BTS is pictured at a 2019 media event in Los Angeles. Personalized social media postings made by the group have helped create a dedicated following of BTS fans known as the BTS Army.

"[BTS knows] how to turn the fan into a super fan, through meaningful, authentic dialogue and how to create a symbiotic relationship between the band and their fan community."[31]

—Mike Schabel, Kiswe CEO

Subscribers can use the app to watch a band-produced series called *Run BTS!* that had over 160 episodes by 2023. The series shows the band hanging out backstage, having tea, and even playing Pictionary. These actions have helped BTS become one of the most successful bands of the twenty-first century. Mike Schabel, CEO of the cloud-streaming tech company Kiswe, says, "[BTS knows] how to turn the fan into a super fan, through meaningful, authentic dialogue and how to create a symbiotic relationship between the band and their fan community."[31]

The Fans Make the Band

Weverse translates all interactions between BTS members and fans, and between fans, into ten languages. A related app called Weply sells exclusive BTS merchandise, from posters to pajamas. Members of the Army who use Weply get first dibs on concert tickets.

More than 35 million members of the Army use Weverse, but the app is not exclusive to BTS. Superfans of Justin Bieber, Ariana Grande, Demi Lovato, and other artists can interact with their favorite stars using Weverse. Mark Mulligan, director of Midia Research, explains the importance of the app: "When you look at technologies like Weverse, they are revolutionary. But they're also simply [promoting] this underlying principle. . . . And that is the idea of nurturing fandom."[32]

Entertainers have been nurturing fandom for decades, but social media platforms have supercharged the process. Fans run news sites about their favorite idols and organize social media campaigns to influence record sales and awards shows. And the wrath of superfans can even serve to impact the actions of corporate behemoths such as Ticketmaster. Although top-selling acts employ dozens of professional marketers, a high level of engagement by superfans can turn any musical act into a multibillion-dollar franchise.

CHAPTER THREE

Favorite Franchises: Film and Television Fandom

The first season of the romantic fantasy series *Bridgerton* began streaming on Netflix in late 2020. The show, set in 1813 during Great Britain's Regency Era, was an instant hit. Netflix says at least 82 million people tuned in to watch Season 1 of *Bridgerton*. When Season 2 dropped in 2022, the show debuted at number one in ninety-two countries.

Bridgerton reimagined the lifestyles of English nobles and royals as they attended lavish parties, engaged in steamy affairs, and searched for respectable marriage partners. As entertainment reporter Wendy Lee writes, *Bridgerton* "can be summed up in one (hyphenated) word: swoon-worthy."[33] The show's swoon-worthy popularity inspired an opulent fashion trend known as Regencycore that highlighted hoop skirts, capes, tiaras, top hats, and tulle.

Taking a page from music idols, Netflix used the *Bridgerton*'s popularity to cultivate a loyal fan base. The streaming network re-created the Regency Era in real-life formal events called "The Queen's Ball: A Bridgerton Experience." In 2022 around eight hundred balls were held in North American cities, including San Francisco, Atlanta, and Montreal. More than 150,000 *Bridgerton* fans attended the balls, most dressed in lavish Regencycore fashions. As might be expected, the balls spawned massive interest online. The events generated more than half a billion social media impressions on Instagram, TikTok, Facebook, and elsewhere. Netflix

A performance artist depicting a bumblebee dances at a Bridgerton ball in Chicago in 2022. Bridgerton balls are just one of a number of live events that Netflix has held for superfans.

entertainment director Greg Lombardo explained the rationale behind the balls: "It's an opportunity for fans to particularly engage with this show. . . . It's a way to have a dialogue with our fans and allow them that moment to not only remember what they love about the show but hopefully remember what they love about Netflix."[34]

The Queen's Ball is just one of the live events Netflix held for superfans. The company also hosted interactive live events for other popular shows, including *Stranger Things* and *Squid Game*. These buzz-worthy happenings, heavily promoted on social media, created interest among those who had not seen the shows when they were originally broadcast. Theater actor Erika Coyne decided to tune into *Bridgerton* after viewing clips of the Queen's Ball on TikTok. "I said, 'OK, there's clearly something very interesting going on here. Everybody wants to go to these balls. It has something to do with "Bridgerton." Let's try and watch it, see if I get hooked by the same thing.' And, of course, I did,"[35] she recalls.

Trekkie Superfans

Although formal balls based on *Bridgerton* are a recent phenomenon, superfans have long obsessed over their favorite television shows and movies. Many trace the phenomenon back to the science fiction television show *Star Trek*, which aired for three seasons in the 1960s on NBC. The show followed a crew of astronauts on the USS *Enterprise* during the twenty-third century. At the beginning of every episode, Captain James T. Kirk, played by William Shatner, said of the *Enterprise*, "Its five-year mission: to explore strange new worlds, to seek out new life and new civilizations, to boldly go where no man has gone before."[36]

Star Trek only aired for three seasons beginning in 1965, but the show gained devoted fans who called themselves Trekkies. They were attracted by the show's distinctive characters, futuristic sets, and visual effects, which were far more advanced than those seen in other sci-fi shows of the era.

Playing *Squid Game* in Real Life

In 2021, the Netflix series *Squid Game* was the network's number one show in ninety-four countries, including the United States. The show revolves around people who are unable to pay off large debts and play children's games, such as tug-of-war, to win cash prizes; however, those who lose are brutally murdered.

The popularity of *Squid Game* prompted Netflix to create an immersive, interactive live game based on the series. Using motion-tracking technology and touch screens that line the walls of digital smart rooms called Gameboxes, groups of two to six people compete in challenges like those featured on the show. The virtual lives of those who lose *Squid Game* are terminated. Winners earn virtual money. "For me, the best part of the experience was getting to see aspects of the show in person," writes superfan Hannah Sacks. "As someone who binge-watched the entire show in less than a week, it was cool to be able to play out some of the scenarios that I watched my favorite characters go through. Of course, we get the better end of the deal—with no repercussions, we can play the game AND have a good time."

Hannah Sacks, "Think You Can Survive 'Squid Game'? We Played it IRL at Immersive Gamebox," *Pop Insider*, September 22, 2022. https://thepopinsider.com.

Star Trek was also one of the most diverse shows on television at the time. Major characters included a Black female communications officer played by Nichelle Nichols and a Japanese American helmsman played by George Takei. Although *Star Trek* never attracted a huge audience, Trekkies remained deeply committed to the show, especially to Spock, the half-human, half-Vulcan science officer played by Leonard Nimoy. The first *Star Trek* fanzine (fan magazine), published in 1967, was called *Spockanalia*.

When NBC tried to cancel *Star Trek* after the second season due to low ratings, a Trekkie named Betty JoAnne "Bjo" Trimble initiated a "Save *Star Trek*" letter-writing campaign. This is believed to have been the first time that fans worked together to keep a television show on the air. NBC gave in to pressure and produced another season.

Famous Trekkies

The *Star Trek* franchise has produced several generations of Trekkies, including numerous famous fans, such as actors Olivia Wilde and Rosario Dawson, musician Rihanna, and former president Barack Obama. In the case of life imitating art, the man who developed the first mobile phone, Martin Cooper, said his invention was inspired by the handheld communicators used on *Star Trek*. Computer engineer Steve Wozniak is a Trekkie who attended *Star Trek* conventions as a kid. The advanced science in the show inspired Wozniak to cofound Apple, one of the most successful tech companies in the world. Other famous scientists and engineers who are Trekkies include the late physicist Stephen Hawking, astrophysicist Neil deGrasse Tyson, Amazon founder Jeff Bezos, Tesla CEO and Space X founder Elon Musk, and scientist and television host Bill Nye. Employees of the National Aeronautics and Space Administration (NASA) have also honored *Star Trek*. The agency has a web page dedicated to connections between NASA designs and those seen on the television show. As NASA astronaut Victor Glover stated in the documentary *NASA on the Edge of Forever: Science in Space*, "Science and *Star Trek* go hand-in-hand."

Quoted in Kelli Mars, "50 Years of NASA and Star Trek Connections," National Aeronautics and Space Administration, June 6, 2019. www.nasa.gov.

Star Trek was canceled in 1969, but the show never disappeared; reruns were shown in the United States and in sixty other countries throughout the 1970s. And the number of Trekkies continued to grow. The first major *Star Trek* convention was held in New York City in 1972. Although the small group of Trekkie organizers expected a few hundred fans to attend, several thousand people showed up. They were able to view *Star Trek* artwork, participate in a costume contest, and watch episodes on a big screen in an auditorium. In the subsequent years, *Star Trek* conventions attracted original cast members, including Nimoy, Takei, Nichols, and Shatner.

The popularity of *Star Trek* gave birth to a long-running franchise that consisted of a string of television series that stretched from *The Next Generation* (1987–1994) to *Strange New Worlds* in 2022. Since 1979, thirteen films have been based on the series. And the franchise has had a huge cultural impact that influenced the lives of millions of fans, including some of the world's leading scientists, engineers, and astronauts.

More than fifty years after the first convention, Trekkies continue to gather and celebrate *Star Trek*. In 2023 *Star Trek* conventions were held in California, Nevada, Texas, and other states. There are countless fan groups on social media and endless forums in which Trekkie-related subjects are debated. And some superfans show their love for *Star Trek* with a dedication not seen elsewhere. One of those fans, James Cawley, obtained blueprints and drawings in 1997 that were used to build the original *Star Trek* television stage set. Cawley went on to spend over $100,000 to build exact replicas of Captain Kirk's bridge, engine room, and sick bay in an abandoned car dealership in Port Henry, New York. In 2004 Cawley and dozens of other superfans began using the set to produce a fan-created web series called *Star Trek: New Voyages*. By 2017 Cawley had produced eleven full-length films. The series continues to pull in fans on YouTube, where *Star Trek: New Voyages* had attracted over 1 million views by 2023.

Fans Love Star Wars

The *Star Trek* franchise is responsible for several books, magazines, games, video games, toys, and comics. The show is also said to have inspired *Star Trek*'s biggest competitor, *Star Wars*, which has also had a major cultural impact. The *Star Wars* franchise, produced by George Lucas, was launched in 1977 with *Episode IV: The New Hope*. Almost since the film debuted, diehard *Star Wars* fans followed the franchise through more than ten blockbuster films and five popular television series. Fans on social media discuss the exact specifications of the spacecraft *Millennium Falcon* featured in the series and arrange get-togethers to watch movie marathons.

In 2019, the Fandom website, which has more than 300 million monthly users, decided to study the habits of *Star Wars* fans on its platform. According to Fandom, more than half of *Star Wars* lovers consider themselves to be extremely dedicated fans of the

Star Wars superfan Dave Oldbury, pictured here in 2015, spent thousands of dollars on his merchandise collection. That year, he offered other fans the chance to stay at his home in Southampton, in the United Kingdom, where he kept his Star Wars memorabilia.

franchise. Around two-thirds of the superfans own *Star Wars* toys, collectibles, and video games. Around one-quarter say they have created original *Star Wars* fan fiction or video content, and one-third had dressed up as a *Star Wars* character. And whereas regular *Star Wars* fans spent an average of $1,032 over the life of the franchise, superfans have doled out nearly $2,900.

Supernatural Fangirls

An untold number of superfans write fan fiction based on their most beloved shows, but Katherine Larsen and Lynn S. Zubernis wrote and published an entire book about their fandom. *Fangasm* describes their obsessive love for the television series *Supernatural*, which ran from 2005 to 2020. The sci-fi show follows two handsome brothers, Sam (played by Jared Padalecki) and Dean Winchester (Jensen Ackles), as they travel America and hunt demons.

Dedicated fans of shows such as *Supernatural* are often stereotyped as fanatical teens, but Larsen is an English literature professor and Zubernis is a psychologist. But in 2013 Larsen's and Zubernis's fandom found them taking a break from their jobs. They were standing in line at the San Diego Comic-Con fan convention at 4 a.m. They had spent thousands of dollars on plane tickets, lodging, meals, a car rental, and tickets to Comic-Con to get a good seat at a 3 p.m. *Supernatural* panel discussion featuring the show's hunky stars.

Larsen and Zubernis met a superfan who claimed Ackles was her true soulmate. Another fan offered a thousand-dollar reward for a coffee cup Padalecki had tossed out at the convention. Although some might wonder about the sanity of these die-hard *Supernatural* devotees, Larsen and Zubernis suggest that the usual reason people latch on to a television show or actor is because many superfans feel like social outsiders who find a sense of belonging within the fan community. But fandom is not always logical, according to Larsen and Zubernis. They argue,

Only once in a while does something grab you so completely that the word "obsession" starts to seem appropriate. Rationally, we knew there were explanations for why we suddenly fell down the rabbit hole of *Supernatural* fandom. None of these theories mattered to us at the time. Falling into fandom is like falling in love. We don't always make the smartest choices or make those choices for the best of reasons. . . . Decisions are made with the gut, not the head. We were simply hooked.[37]

Obsessed by Game of Thrones

Supernatural superfans might be dedicated, but according to a 2022 IMDb poll, those who love *Game of Thrones* are the most obsessive fans of any television series. *Game of Thrones*, based on a series of fantasy novels by George R.R. Martin, ran for eight seasons beginning in 2011. The HBO series focuses on the bloody conflicts between noble families who lived on the imaginary continents of Westeros and Essos. *Game of Thrones* attracted a record-setting audience and is responsible for fueling an international fan base that continued after the show concluded in 2019.

Game of Thrones has generated a massive number of fan fiction stories. The fan fiction website Archive of Our Own lists nearly sixty-thousand works based on the series. Stories range from a few paragraphs to nearly one hundred thousand words. Fan art for the show is also popular; the online arts and crafts marketplace Etsy lists nearly nine hundred sellers offering everything from *Game of Thrones* T-shirts to themed stickers, paintings, and jewelry. Media blogger Nia writes, "Fandoms are at the center of transformative works. . . . The fan art community, for instance, takes pop culture stories and extends those characters into new adventures, absurdities, and unexpected relationships. Most young people's creative processes start in fan

> "The fan art community . . . takes pop culture stories and extends those characters into new adventures, absurdities, and unexpected relationships."[38]
>
> —Nia, media blogger

art and are only limited by the imagination of the artist."[38]

"The biggest take away from any convention: the memories are the best part."[39]

—Camila Servello, *Game of Thrones* fan

The imaginations of fan artists were on display at the first official *Game of Thrones* fan convention held in 2022 at the Los Angeles Convention Center. Fans were treated to panel discussions, photo ops with the show's stars, autograph sessions, and a dance party. *Game of Thrones* superfan Camila Servello reviewed the convention for the FanSided website, saying, "It was a truly great weekend, with experiences I know I'll never forget. It was worth the cross-country trip for me, and I made some heavy purchases, but the cast's answers to all of my questions . . . will always stick with me. And that's the biggest take away from any convention: the memories are the best part."[39]

The most devoted *Game of Thrones* fans preserved their memories by naming their children after characters in the show. According to the Social Security Administration, which tracks baby names, between 2011 and 2019 more than ten thousand

A Game of Thrones *fan watches the show on a laptop. Digital culture allows fans to do things like rewatch old episodes or talk about characters with other fans, any time or day that they want.*

newborns were bestowed with *Game of Thrones* character names, including Khaleesi, Arya, Daenerys, Sansa, and Samwell.

The Journey to Superfandom

The rise of the superfan is a relatively new phenomenon fueled by the internet. During the 1960s, *Star Trek* enthusiasts had to wait for a new episode to air each week and find one another through fanzines or sporadic conventions. Today, digital fan culture is on all day, every day. Fans can rewatch old episodes on streaming sites, share ideas, argue over obscure references, and participate in their own stories inspired by their favorite shows. And anyone who becomes a dedicated superfan is embarking on a journey. From binge-watching an entire series to traveling across the country for a convention to naming a child after a favorite character, the life of a fan might have as many twists and turns as an episode of *Game of Thrones*. As Larsen and Zubernis write, "Once you're hooked you want more. More information, more pictures, more viewings, more of everything associated with the show."[40]

CHAPTER FOUR

Heroes and Villains: Comics and Anime Fandom

Sheldon Dorf might be considered one of the most committed comic book superfans. Born in 1933, Dorf was fascinated by the comics of the era, such as *Superman* and *Batman*. Dorf loved comics and comic books so much that in 1970 he organized the first comic book convention, the Golden State Comic-Con in San Diego. Dorf was surprised when more than three hundred fans turned up to talk about their favorite characters, meet with comic creators, and swap comic books. One of the featured guests was legendary comic book artist Jack Kirby, who, with Stan Lee, cocreated superhero stories featuring the Fantastic Four, X-Men, and Hulk. The event was renamed San Diego Comic-Con in 1973. Since that time, the gathering has grown into the world's largest convention for superfans of comics, animation, Japanese-style manga and anime, and live-action films based on comics. Similar conventions are held in major cities throughout the world, including New York, Toronto, Tokyo, and Paris.

In 2022 around 150,000 people attended San Diego Comic-Con, with many of the attendees wearing costumes of their favorite superheroes, supervillains, and other colorful characters. Among the estimated 15,000 cosplayers, Wonder Woman, the Joker, Harley Quinn, and Spider-Man were among the most popular. The halls of Comic-Con also include a profusion of cosplayers dressed as Japanese anime characters, including heroes such as Monkey D. Luffy of *One Piece* and evildoers such as Akaza from *Demon Slayer*.

Cosplay is a combination of the words "costume play." The term was coined in 1984 when Japanese studio head Nobuyuki Takahashi attended the World Science Fiction Convention in Los Angeles. Takahashi was amazed when he saw hundreds of people wearing costumes of their favorite characters from Japanese manga and anime. Since then, cosplay has become a favorite activity of dedicated fans of all types of comics and animation, especially at comic conventions.

Cosplayers who make their own costumes spend hundreds of dollars just for fabric and buttons. It can cost much more to buy wigs, shoes, jewelry, and other accessories. Cosplayers might spend weeks or months sewing together their costumes and perfecting makeup and hairstyles. Attending a hot, crowded convention poses its own problems, especially for cosplayers in full bodysuits who

Fans pose for a picture at the 2019 San Diego Comic-Con. Comic-Con is the world's largest convention for superfans of comics, books, animation, manga and anime, and live-action films based on comics.

need to take extra precautions to stay cool. But cosplay is worth the cost and effort, according to writer Andrea Towers, who loves to portray the Black Widow, a member of the Avengers superhero team. "When I dress up [as Black Widow]," Towers says, "I'm allowed to fully escape from my 'real life' in a way that is special to me and a way that makes me feel empowered. . . . Putting on a costume helps me transform into a person who can take on the world with a different kind of confidence. . . . The time I'm spending in cosplay changes me for the better."[41]

"Putting on a costume helps me transform into a person who can take on the world with a different kind of confidence. . . . The time I'm spending in cosplay changes me for the better."[41]

—Andrea Towers, writer and cosplayer

Cutting Up Naruto

Cosplayers in Japan often engage in a lifestyle known as *otaku* culture. *Otaku* is a Japanese word that describes someone who has an obsessive interest in manga and anime. English terms that correspond to *otaku* are *geek* or *nerd*, but these words often have negative connotations. *Otaku*, on the other hand, has lost its negative meaning in Japan, where it has become a prominent and accepted aspect of modern culture.

The popular anime *Naruto* is an *otaku* favorite. The origins of *Naruto* can be found in a manga written and illustrated by Masashi Kishimoto from 1999 to 2015. The story follows a young, troubled ninja fighter named Naruto Uzumaki, known as the Hero of the Hidden Leaves. Naruto has a powerful life force that gives him superhuman powers, including the ability to summon numerous shadow clones that allow him to conquer enemies. The incredibly complex story of *Naruto* develops over 453 manga chapters and 720 twenty-minute anime episodes produced from 2002 to 2017. Although the story of *Naruto* concluded, the franchise continues to resonate with fans. In 2022 characters such as Naruto and the supervillain Hidan were among the most popular among manga and anime superfans at the Los Angeles Anime Expo.

How Manga Speaks to Fans

Fans have a voracious appetite for manga. One reason for this might be that the stories often reflect their own experiences or appeal to their values. Manga plots tend to focus on universal themes like friendship, love, and the struggle to fit in. Many stories feature young, relatable heroes, including formidable females and LGBTQ characters, who start out as struggling outcasts. These outsiders go on to acquire magical or superhuman powers. This allows them to expose hypocrisy, fight evil, and find romance. When the characters transcend their mundane lives they come to better understand themselves.

Highlighting the experiences and concerns of young people can lead to great success. Few manga creators grasp this dynamic better than Eiichiro Oda who first published *One Piece*, the bestselling manga of all time, in 1997. The action-adventure story about a lovable monkey pirate is still going strong today. Oda's success can be traced to the way he relates to his fans: "Whenever I draw manga, I have only one reader in my mind—myself as a 15-year-old. . . . I turn back to the 15-year-old me to make a judgment on what is awesome or not. I always try to stay true to myself, and somehow it resonates with the kids who read my manga."

Quoted in Misaki C. Kido, "Interview: Eiichiro Oda," Viz, April 2, 2012. www.viz.com.

A superfan who goes by the handle *Oceaniz* loves the *Naruto* anime, but his girlfriend, Laura, was not interested in the series. This inspired Oceaniz to edit down the entire anime series to make it more appealing to Laura. Oceaniz says he created the Ocean Cut of *Naruto* by viewing more than 250 hours of the anime series and removing what he considered unnecessary scenes: "Entire seasons of filler, 10-minute-long flashbacks, literally hundreds of reaction shots. . . . The flashbacks in particular are so bad that certain scenes are shown up to, no joke, 20 different times, with only a fraction of them showing any new information."[42] When the editing process was completed the Ocean Cut of *Naruto* was around 135 hours long.

Oceaniz reviews anime and video games on his YouTube channel, which has more than 143,000 subscribers. In 2022 he uploaded a thirty-minute video that explained how and why he took on the editing project. The video attracted more than 1.3 million views. In the video, Oceaniz says the editing process took around three months, and it was not fun: "Would I ever do this again? Absolutely not. I almost know 'Naruto' by heart and even so, this was an insane amount of work. Doing this for any series I'm less familiar with would be a nightmare."[43] As for Laura, she told Oceaniz, "It was surprisingly one of the best shows you've shown me so far."[44]

Marvel and DC Superfans

The *Naruto* franchise has earned over $10 billion, but this huge sum is only a fraction of the money made by two other companies: Marvel Cinematic Universe and DC Comics. These two entertainment industry powerhouses account for 70 percent of comic book sales every year, and their animated and live-action superhero franchises earn billions of dollars annually.

Marvel and DC have created superheroes that are recognized the world over. Marvel characters include the Hulk, Ant-Man, Iron Man, and Spider-Man, and DC created Superman, Batman, Wonder Woman, and the Green Lantern along with crime-fighting teams such as the Justice League. And both companies have

Spider-Man fans pose during a 2019 fan convention in London. Marvel characters such as Spider-Man are recognized around the world and have inspired many superfans.

multitudes of superfans, according to a 2022 Fandom survey of five thousand entertainment and gaming fans. In the Fandom survey, 81 percent of Marvel fans said they would read or watch anything released by the company, and 66 percent of DC fans said the same. The most intense superhero fans surveyed said they are so deeply committed to their favorite franchise that it is "part of who they are."[45]

In 2022 one of those DC devotees set a record that earned a mention in the Guinness World Records. A seven-year-old child actor from Tamil Nadu, India, known as Nidhish V B, was able to name sixty DC characters in sixty seconds. This beat the previous record of fifty-three set in 2021 by S. Mohammed Harsath. Nidhish woke up at 5 a.m. for over two months to study the stable of DC characters. He said his job memorizing dialog for his role in an Indian soap opera helped him set the record. Nidhish says his favorite character is Batman. "He is strongest of all, he learns from his mistakes and he also has good moral values,"[46] Nidhish says, and he dresses in his black-and-gold Batsuit whenever possible.

Black Panther Forges a New Path

One of the most iconic superhero characters in recent memory was born in 1966 on the pages of the Marvel comic book *Fantastic Four* created by comic book legends Stan Lee and Jack Kirby. Black Panther, or T'Challa, was the first Black superhero ever seen in a mainstream American comic book. T'Challa is the king of a fictional African nation called Wakanda. The king assumes the identity of the superwarrior Black Panther to protect his scientifically advanced society from evil outsiders.

Black Panther later got his own story line in *Panther's Rage*, which is considered the first graphic novel because of its length; it contains a two-hundred-page narrative that runs through thirteen issues (1973–1975). Alex Simmons says he was an instant fan of the Black Panther character when he first appeared. Simmons

Hyperfans Fund Afrocentric Comics

Fandom is often associated with billion-dollar franchises produced by DC Comics and the Marvel Cinematic Universe. But Manuel and Geiszel Godoy understand that dedicated fans can also help small companies succeed. The Godoys founded Black Sands Entertainment (BSE) in 2016 to publish comics and graphic novels created by Black artists. Stories focus on Black heroes, African mythology, and Afrofuturism, a combination of African culture, history, mythology, and innovative technology.

Black Sands was powered by fans from the start. The company initially raised $20,000 with a Kickstarter campaign, which allowed them to publish their first comics. The Godoys turned to social media to enlarge their fan base and promote new offerings. Manuel says he is a fan of manga and anime, which inspired the way BSE relates to fans: "You're not supposed to reach everyone. [We] don't try to make something for 17 different audiences. . . . In the West, everyone wants to be so big. In [Japan], a million hyperfans are more valuable than 20 million [casual readers]."

In 2022 hyperfans helped BSE raise over $1 million on the Wefunder platform. Those who contributed received a small stake in the company; 15 percent of BSE is now owned by fans.

Quoted in S. Mitra Kalita, "Lessons for Entrepreneurs from the Comic-Book Startup Reframing Black History," *Charter*, June 14, 2022. https://time.com.

went on to write stories for a number of comic books, including *Blackjack*. Simmons explains why T'Challa was important to so many fans like him:

> T'Challa, the Black Panther . . . is ethical, and vulnerable, and committed to his people and to a code moral or otherwise. He will sacrifice himself for the greater good. These are admirable traits in anyone, and yes they existed in Black people throughout history, but the population of this planet has been systematically starved of such images. Up until this character appeared in popular fiction one had to dig deep into family tales and specifically generated publications for Blacks and African Americans to find anything about characters like this.[47]

Wakanda Forever

Legions of new T'Challa fans were minted after Marvel released the live-action film *Black Panther* in 2018. Journalist Rivea Ruff writes, "[*Black Panther*] was something of a family event for Black Americans in particular. We descended on theaters multiple times in droves, dressed in Afrocentric chic to take in the story of T'Challa and the mythical kingdom of Wakanda."[48]

This picture shows a poster from the 2022 movie, Wakanda Forever, *which is the sequel to* Black Panther. *Fans have praised these movies for their depiction of Afrofuturism.*

Fans praised the movie for its depiction of Afrofuturism, which melds African culture, mythology, and futuristic technology. And *Black Panther* presented numerous characters, besides T'Challa, that drew in fans. Erik "Killmonger" Stevens, portrayed by Michael B. Jordan, is one of the best—or worst—supervillains in all comic book movie history. Jordan won numerous awards for his role, including a Teen Choice Award for Choice Villain.

"I got a lot of messages, especially from young women, who were so happy to see themselves on screen [as Shuri in Black Panther], they were so happy to see someone making science and technology cool."[49]

—Letitia Wright, actor

Black Panther also featured female characters that were credited with making the film a success. The character Shuri, played by Letitia Wright, is a princess and a scientific mastermind who engineers high-tech gear for the people of Wakanda. As Wright said in 2018, "I got a lot of messages, especially from young women, who were so happy to see themselves on screen, they were so happy to see someone making science and technology cool."[49]

The *Black Panther* sequel, *Wakanda Forever* debuted in 2022 in more than forty-five hundred theaters, earning record profits. But the joy of fans was mixed with sadness. Chadwick Boseman, the actor who played T'Challa in *Black Panther*, had died of cancer in 2020. Without showing the character, T'Challa's demise was part of the story line in the sequel. During the opening weekend of *Wakanda Forever*, fans dressed in white to honor the star. Ruff explains that it was a "way to 'participate' in the character's on-screen funeral procession."[50]

Worldwide Fandom

It is easy to see why superfans love superheroes. In an uncertain world marked by war, natural disasters, and other tragedies, superhero stories offer a temporary break from the onslaught of bad news. Superheroes are brave and true and show a willingness to lay their lives on the line for regular folks. With their heroic deeds, they exhibit superhuman compassion that sets a good example for fans who hope to lead righteous lives. Of course, some love

"Villains can be very colorful characters. . . . They are charismatic
and smart. [They] go outside the
boundaries of acceptable society,
and that appeals to those who
would want to break from the
mold."[51]

—Rich Tanari, costume salesperson

supervillains whose larger-than-life personalities and iconic looks act as a magnet for cosplayers, fan fiction writers, and other superfans. Costume salesperson Rich Tanari explains, "Villains can be very colorful characters. . . . They are charismatic and smart. [They] go outside the boundaries of acceptable society, and that appeals to those who would want to break from the mold."[51]

Love of supervillains and superheroes is not limited to North America. Franchises based on Black Panther, Batman, Spider-Man, and the Joker attract millions of fans in China, Germany, Italy, Mexico, and elsewhere. And with the Marvel Cinematic Universe and DC Comics leading the way, fans and die-hard devotees will never run out of ways to stoke their superfandom.

CHAPTER FIVE

Team Loyalty: Sports and E-sports Fandom

In 2022 major professional sports leagues in the United States brought in nearly $70 billion. This huge sum was generated in part by superfans who make football, basketball, baseball, soccer, and other sports part of their daily lives. Beyond creating massive profits, sports play a much deeper role in society, according to sports analysts Ben Valenta and David Sikorjak: "Sports fandom is a social superconductor, enabling fans to make meaningful connections not only across entrenched team loyalties but across social categories such as race, class, religion, gender, generation and, yes, even politics."[52]

Valenta and Sikorjak describe how sports acted as a social superconductor for a man referred to as Marco who immigrated to the United States from Italy during the 2000s. Like most Europeans, Marco was a soccer fan but paid little attention to American sports. After landing a job in New York City, Marco began accompanying his coworkers to most home games played by the New York Yankees. This placed him on what Valenta and Sikorjak describe as the fandom flywheel: "Essentially, you lean into your fandom, you participate in fan activities, you engage as a fan. . . . And that creates the positive feedback of social interactions . . . which incentivizes you to lean into more fan activities, more fan engagement, which only then begets more social interaction. Once it starts to spin, it takes over."[53]

The Fandom Flywheel

Propelled by the positive feedback from coworkers, Marco began following football. He joined a fantasy football league, which he was managing by 2018. Marco says that managing a fantasy football league was a huge commitment but one that provided benefits. "It was a big opportunity for me to get closer to other people, to have something in common to talk about,"[54] he explains. As the fandom flywheel continued to spin, Marco developed a passion for golf. This brought him closer to a different group of work friends, who often gathered to watch tournaments on television.

Citing Marco's experience in becoming a more committed sports fan over the years, Valenta and Sikorjak write, "This fly-

A fan plays fantasy football on an iPhone. Many people find that fantasy sports are a good way to connect with other fans.

wheel we're talking about—it's not trivial. It doesn't merely pull you into buying jerseys, or watching more games, or deepening your sports knowledge (although it does do those things). It pulls you into initiating more social interactions. And that, we suspect, is where the real payoff lies."[55] According to Valenta and Sikorjak, more social interaction creates a greater sense of well-being and happiness in sports fans along with higher levels of optimism, gratitude, and confidence.

The social interaction of devoted fans provides entrance to a world where detailed knowledge of each play, player, and game can provide hours of entertainment. As blogger Hari Dandapani writes,

> Once you've bought into a sports universe, the potential for analysis is endless. Sports fans spend their time arguing over who the greatest of all time (GOAT) is. They invest themselves in . . . [upholding] long-running rivalries with other fan communities who have constructed different stories and assigned different protagonists and antagonists from the same set of events. These points of discussion—which may seem mundane to outsiders—are how sports fans construct the narratives that keep them so excited. . . . They know what good dunks, clutch touchdowns, and crazy knuckleballs look like—these are things they've seen before. What they want is a good story.[56]

Never Missed a Game

Steve Young knows all about the best dunks, touchdowns, and knuckleballs—at least those delivered by high school kids who play on local teams in his Chicago suburb. In 2022 Young was a ninety-one-year-old high school sports superfan who lived in Antioch, Illinois. Young had never missed a single Antioch Community High School football game since 1946. He also attended nearly every Antioch basketball game, softball game, and volleyball game. According to Young's count, he attends matches, tournaments, and games in more than twenty sports, including tennis, golf, and bowling.

Young is such a sports superfan that he did not miss a single football game—even after he got into a serious car accident in a severe thunderstorm when he was in his seventies. "I had 11 broken bones, punctured left lung and while I was laying on the stretcher, I got hit by lightning. Knocked me off the stretcher," Young said. "They got me in the hospital and one doctor says, 'He's not going to make it.' And I said, 'You guys don't know what you're talking about. I've got a game to go to!'"[57] Several weeks later, Young attended the Antioch season opener.

Young is a familiar sight to those who see him at home and away games. Sometimes the high school players tell Young he is the only person they know at a game; their parents are too busy to attend. In 2022 Antioch students thanked Young. He was appointed grand marshal of the homecoming parade and was honored at a game when the crowd cheered loudly for the sports fan with the perfect seventy-six-year attendance record.

Standing Out in the Crowd

Young's devotion to high school sports makes him instantly recognizable to three generations of Antioch residents. But superfans who seek recognition in stadiums holding as many as a hundred thousand people have a harder time standing out in the crowd. This has not been a problem for Boston Red Sox superfan Mike Schuster, who attracts plenty of attention for his outrageous outfits when he attends games in Fenway Park. Schuster says he has been a Red Sox fanatic since 1975 and has lost track of how many baseball games he has attended. But whenever Schuster goes to Fenway Park, he turns heads with a huge Red Sox logo painted on his ample belly and his clothing emblazoned with team logos. Schuster's devotion brought him a little fame in 2005. He had a cameo appearance in the baseball movie *Fever Pitch* starring Jimmy Fallon and Drew Barrymore.

Spending Millions on Memorabilia

Many sports enthusiasts spend money on collectibles ranging from bobbleheads to blankets, T-shirts and caps. But some are willing to spend millions on sports memorabilia that have been autographed by their favorite players or even worn during a game. In 2022 a jersey worn by basketball great Michael Jordan during the 1998 NBA finals sold for $10.1 million. This surpassed the previous record, set only a few months earlier, of $9.2 million paid for the jersey worn by soccer legend Diego Maradona during the 1986 World Cup. Superfans have also paid huge sums for jerseys worn by hockey legend Wayne Gretzky and football icon Tom Brady.

Collecting baseball cards is a tradition for many kids, but values for the most collectible cards have skyrocketed in recent years. In 2022 a seventy-year-old Mickey Mantle baseball card sold for $12.6 million. The card was previously owned by New York Yankees superfan Anthony Giordano, who had bought it in 1991 for $50,000. Meanwhile, a basketball card autographed by LeBron James brought in $5.2 million. And James has so many superfans that some of his older basketball cards are worth even more. According to memorabilia expert Jesse Craig, "There are LeBron cards [still] out there . . . worth over $10 million."

Quoted in ESPN, "The Most Expensive Sports Memorabilia and Collectibles in History," September 15, 2022. www.espn.com.

Schuster is also a New England Patriots football superfan. His first job was selling hot dogs, peanuts, and soda at Patriots games. He began purchasing season tickets and even bought a home within walking distance of Gillette Stadium, home to the Patriots. Schuster explains, "When I got season tickets I vowed to shave my head and have it painted to look like a Patriots helmet the next time the Patriots made the Superbowl; of course I kept my word."[58]

Cleveland Guardians baseball fan John Adams did not need to shave his head to get attention. During baseball season, Adams could be seen—and heard—at Cleveland's Progressive Field pounding on a big bass drum. Adams

> "I vowed to shave my head and have it painted to look like a Patriots helmet the next time the Patriots made the Superbowl; of course I kept my word."[58]
>
> —Mike Schuster, New England Patriots superfan

was first inspired to make a lot of noise when the team played at Cleveland's old Municipal Stadium. Fans following a tradition, pounded on the wooden seats during exciting moments in the game. But Adams preferred to sit in the bleachers, where there were no individual seats to bang. In 1973 he bought a cheap bass drum at a garage sale and started beating on it when a game started, when a player was close to scoring, and at the end of every game. A local reporter asked Adams to attend every game with his drum—and he did. Adams was at every home game between 1973 and 2019.

Adams has been honored for his fandom in a few ways. He provided inspiration for the drummers in *Major League*, a 1989 sports comedy about a fictionalized version of the Cleveland baseball team. In 2006 the team dedicated a bobblehead night to Adams. And Adams was selected several times to throw out the ceremonial first pitch. Adams was often the only person sitting in the last row of the bleachers in Progressive Stadium. When he died in 2023, his drum mallets were displayed at the

This photo shows a baseball game between the Boston Red Sox and the Minnesota Twins at Fenway Park in Boston, Massachusetts. Baseball superfans can have trouble standing out in stadiums that hold tens of thousands of people.

Superfan Re-creates a Video Game at Home

The medieval role-playing video game *The Elder Scrolls* has millions of fans. But few are more dedicated to the game than Tyler Kirkham, who enjoys the role-playing game because "you are the character and you're essentially living the life of this character in a fantasy world," he says. Love of this fantasy world prompted Kirkham to spend over $50,000 to re-create the world of *The Elder Scrolls* in his basement.

Kirkham is a California-based artist whose day job consists of drawing DC Comics. His work can be seen in *The Amazing Spider Man*, *Batman: Black and White*, *Green Lantern Corps*, and other publications. Kirkham's artistic flair is on display in his basement fantasy world. The room, modeled on the tavern in *The Elder Scrolls*, is filled with replica furniture. Medieval helmets, armor, swords, axes, and an antique Italian crossbow are readily available. The $15,000 bathroom, based on the game, was built to look like a mineshaft, complete with water dripping down the stone walls. According to Kirkham, "Being able to get online and play with my friends who are miles away or even countries away is amazing to me. . . . That excites me a lot about *The Elder Scrolls*."

Quoted in Russell Nickerson, "Ultimate Man Cave $50,000 Elder Scrolls Basement," YouTube, 2018. www.youtube.com/watch?v=QqOTGRRc27Q.

National Baseball Hall of Fame and Museum in Cooperstown, New York. He is one of the few superfans to be honored by the museum.

Leagues of E-sports Superfans

Professional sports leagues have long attracted legions of committed fans who make rooting for their team the central focus of their lives. But superfans of a new generation are switching off football, basketball, and other professional sports to watch other people play video games.

Electronic sports, or e-sports, have grown into a multibillion-dollar international industry with viewership that now rivals traditional sports. According to Statista.com, more than half a billion people worldwide followed e-sports in 2022, and around 271 million considered themselves e-sports enthusiasts or superfans.

Team Liquid competes at a League of Legends championship in Berlin, Germany in 2019. The League of Legends World Championship attracts more fans than many major traditional sporting events like the World Series.

Every week millions of e-sports enthusiasts watch professional gamers play multiplayer video game competitions live-streamed on YouTube and Twitch. As with traditional sports, there are franchised e-sports leagues with teams populated by professional players. Winners participate in postseason playoffs that can attract widespread attention. The combined in-person attendance and live-stream viewership for the world championship of the battle arena game *League of Legends* (*LOL*) attracts more fans than major traditional sporting events such as the National Basketball Association (NBA) finals, the World Series, and the Stanley Cup hockey playoffs. Although *LOL* is one of the world's most popular e-sports franchises, others include *Dota*, *Counter-Strike*, *Super Smash Brothers*, and *Street Fighter*.

Like most superfans, those who are devoted to e-sports show their team spirit by donning colorful costumes, painting their faces, and following their favorite players on social media. Some even decorate their homes to look like scenes in their favorite video games. Blogger Dandapani developed a love for e-sports at an early age; he was in fifth grade when he began playing *LOL* online in 2012. He became obsessed with the game and quickly discovered an endless stream of *LOL* content on YouTube. Soon he was hooked on watching live games played on the professional e-sports circuit.

Dandapani later described this period of his life. Every Friday after school he watched games previously played by the European professional *LOL* franchise. He then caught up on highlights from other games he missed, taking breaks only to walk his dog and eat. At night, he fell asleep listening to his favorite streamers on his phone as they played *LOL*. Dandapani picks up the story:

> I awaken refreshed at noon on Saturday. . . . Now, it's time for the North American League. I don my Team Liquid shirt to show support for my favorite team and spend the next five hours watching regular season games. After each game, I switch browser tabs to Reddit to comment my analysis of the winning team's strategy, rewatch the sickest plays, and upvote memes about the day's games. I know all of the players, all of their current and former team affiliations, and all of the narratives surrounding the players and the teams—I am living the life of a League of Legends superfan.[59]

Dandapani's love of *LOL* did not distract him from his studies; he attended Brown University in Rhode Island in 2023. And Dandapani was still an *LOL* superfan. He said excitement associated with the game never gets old, and the game continues to captivate him.

"I know all of the [e-sports] players, all of their current and former team affiliations, and all of the narratives surrounding the players and the teams—I am living the life of a League of Legends superfan."[59]

—Hari Dandapani, blogger

A Nation That Loves Sports

Every superfan has a personal story about their initial commitment to fandom. E-sports fans like Dandapani are often players themselves. But traditional sports fans are often shaped by childhood memories, such as watching games with family members. Others are attracted to game-day excitement and the suspense of each play. And, as with other types of fandom, sports and e-sports are inclusive. Anyone can cheer on a team and enjoy the camaraderie whatever their age, background, or physical abilities. And sports superfans are accepted and honored in almost every segment of culture and society. As sports journalist George Dohrmann writes,

> "We are now clearly a nation of people in intense relationships with our favorite sports teams."[60]
>
> —George Dohrmann, sports journalist

> The importance of having allegiance to a sports team has been reinforced and heightened, to the point that it comes up on first dates and during job interviews and in almost any setting where we are asked to define ourselves. For many people, a fan group has usurped church membership or another community organization as the primary binding agent in our lives. We are now clearly a nation of people in intense relationships with our favorite sports teams."[60]

SOURCE NOTES

Introduction: Fandom and Fan Culture

1. Meredith Hrebenak, "Supernatural: The Power of Fandom for Mental Health," Progressive Counseling Services, November 16, 2022. www.meredithlpc.com.
2. Quoted in Natalie Marchant, "Taxonomy: Why 19 Ferns Are Named After Lady Gaga and a Bug Is Named After Brad Pitt," World Economic Forum, June 14, 2021. www.weforum.org.
3. Joe Coscarelli, "How Pop Music Fandom Became Sports, Politics, Religion, and All-Out War," *New York Times*, December 25, 2020. www.nytimes.com.
4. Quoted in Coscarelli, "How Pop Music Fandom Became Sports, Politics, Religion, and All-Out War."

Chapter One: The Growth of Online Fan Culture

5. Quoted in Claire Murphy, "How Superfans of Harry Styles, Taylor Swift, Billie Eilish & More Are Changing Artist Merchandising with Consumable Fan Art," Recording Academy Grammy Awards, June 1, 2022. www.grammy.com.
6. Quoted in Murphy, "How Superfans of Harry Styles, Taylor Swift, Billie Eilish & More Are Changing Artist Merchandising with Consumable Fan Art."
7. Kaitlyn Tiffany, "How Deadheads and Directioners Made the Internet What It Is Today," Pitchfork, June 7, 2022. https://pitchfork.com.
8. Quoted in Tiffany, "How Deadheads and Directioners Made the Internet What It Is Today."
9. Quoted in Tiffany, "How Deadheads and Directioners Made the Internet What It Is Today."
10. Quoted in Laura Miller, "The New Powers That Be," *Slate*, September 11, 2016. https://slate.com.
11. Quoted in David D. Kirkpatrick, "Harry Potter and the Quest for the Unfinished Volume," *New York Times*, May 5, 2002. www.nytimes.com.
12. Miller, "The New Powers That Be."
13. Nilay Patel, "How Fandom Built the Internet as We Know It, with Kaitlyn Tiffany," The Verge, June 14, 2022. www.theverge.com.
14. Quoted in Patel, "How Fandom Built the Internet as We Know It, with Kaitlyn Tiffany."

15. Quoted in Edward M. Druce, "The Power of the 'Super-Fan': How One Direction Took Over the World (& Lessons in Talent Management)," Medium, November 5, 2017. https://edwarddruce.medium.com.

16. Quoted in Douglas Greenwood, "How One Direction Became the World's First Internet Boy Band," *The Independent* (London), July 23, 2020. www.independent.co.uk.

17. Quoted in Greenwood, "How One Direction Became the World's First Internet Boy Band."

18. Aja Romano, "Fandom Went Mainstream in the 2010s—for Better and Worse," Vox, December 30, 2019. www.vox.com.

19. Miller, "The New Powers That Be."

Chapter Two: Pop Idols: Music Fandom

20. Quoted in Molly Creeden, "Harry Styles Ate Here. His Fans Will Now Eat Here Forever," *New York Times*, February 4, 2023. www.nytimes.com.

21. Quoted in Zack O'Malley Greenberg, "Justin Bieber on the Business of Social Media," *Forbes*, June 22, 2012. www.forbes.com.

22. Luca Macera, "Justin Bieber: Has the World Talking Without Even Trying," Medium, April 2, 2017. https://medium.com.

23. Donna Wells, "3 Personal Branding Lessons from Taylor Swift, Adele, and Other Musicians," Inc., January 14, 2016. www.inc.com.

24. Chloe Melas, "Taylor Swift Releases Short Film That Fans Think Is About Her Ex-Boyfriend Jake Gyllenhaal," CNN, November 13, 2021. www.cnn.com.

25. Quoted in Britney Nguyen, "Ticketmaster Expected 1.5 Million 'Verified' Taylor Swift Fans on the Site but 14 million People Were Trying to Get Tickets, Live Nation Chairman Says: 'We Could Have Filled 900 Stadiums,'" Insider, November 17, 2022. www.businessinsider.com.

26. Eli Motycka and Hannah Herner, "Taylor Swift Ticket Debacle Breaks the Internet," Nashville Scene, November 18, 2022. www.nashvillescene.com.

27. Quoted in August Brown, "How Ticketmaster Became the Most Hated Name in Music," *Los Angeles Times*, January 23, 2023. www.latimes.com.

28. Quoted in August Brown, "Ticketmaster Gets a Bipartisan Grilling on Capitol Hill," *Los Angeles Times*, January 24, 2023. www.latimes.com.

29. E. Alex Jung, "40,000 BTS Fans Can't Be Wrong," *Vulture*, October 10, 2018. www.vulture.com.

30. Quoted in Claire Dodson, "BTS's New Album 'Love Yourself: Tear' Is Out, and the BTS Army Is Already Picking Favorites," *Teen Vogue*, May 18, 2018. www.teenvogue.com.
31. Quoted in Amy Farley, "How the BTS ARMY Turned Their Fandom into the Future of Entertainment," *Fast Company*, March 8, 2022. www.fastcompany.com.
32. Quoted in Farley, "How the BTS ARMY Turned Their Fandom into the Future of Entertainment."

Chapter Three: Favorite Franchises: Film and Television Fandom

33. Wendy Lee, "Taking Its Shows to the Real World, Netflix Invites You to the 'Bridgerton' Ball," *Los Angeles Times*, November 14, 2022. www.latimes.com.
34. Quoted in Lee, "Taking Its Shows to the Real World, Netflix Invites You to the 'Bridgerton' Ball."
35. Quoted in Lee, "Taking Its Shows to the Real World, Netflix Invites You to the 'Bridgerton' Ball."
36. Quoted in Fandom, "*Star Trek* Opening Title Sequence." https://memory-alpha.fandom.com.
37. Katherine Larsen and Lynn S. Zubernis, *Fangasm*. Iowa City: University of Iowa Press, 2013, p. 29.
38. Nia, "The Rise of Fandoms," Medium, November 1, 2019. https://medium.com.
39. Camila Servello, "Review: The First Game of Thrones Official Fan Convention," FanSided, December 14, 2022. https://winteriscoming.net.
40. Larsen and Zubernis, *Fangasm*, p. 32.

Chapter Four: Heroes and Villains: Comics and Anime Fandom

41. Andrea Towers, "Cosplay and Conventions; How Being a Fan Helped Me Rediscover Myself," Popverse, September 21, 2022. www.thepopverse.com.
42. Quoted in Rebecca Moon, "'Naruto' Fan Edits Out 115 Hours of Filler from the Series' 720 Episodes for His Girlfriend," NextShark, April 8, 2022. https://nextshark.com.
43. Oceaniz, "I Re-edited ALL of Naruto for My Girlfriend," April 6, 2022. www.youtube.com/watch?v=II5t9fuUW70&t=11s.
44. Quoted in Oceaniz, "I Re-edited ALL of Naruto for my Girlfriend," April 6, 2022. www.youtube.com/watch?v=II5t9fuUW70&t=11s.
45. Quoted in Adam B. Vary, "Marvel Fans Showing Franchise Fatigue, While DC Fans More Likely to Prefer Single Superhero over Universe, Says New Fandom Study," *Variety*, November 17, 2022. https://variety.com.

46. Quoted in Sanj Atwai, "DC Comics Superfan Names 60 Characters in 60 Seconds," Guinness World Records, March 25, 2022. https://kids.guinnessworldrecords.com.
47. Quoted in Ben Morse, "Alex Simmons on the History of Black Panther," Marvel, February 26, 2021. www.marvel.com.
48. Rivea Ruff, "What 'Wakanda Forever' Means for Marvel Fans," *Essence*, November 14, 2022. www.essence.com.
49. Quoted in Rachel Thompson, "How Shuri from 'Black Panther' Is Inspiring Young Women in STEM," Mashable, June 29, 2018. https://mashable.com.
50. Ruff, "What 'Wakanda Forever' Means for Marvel Fans."
51. Quoted in Victoria Rosenthal, "Villains Reign: Why the Bad Guys Are Getting All the Glory," Pop Insider, July 18, 2019. https://thepopinsider.com.

Chapter Five: Team Loyalty: Sports and E-sports Fandom

52. Ben Valenta and David Sikorjak, "Put Football on Your Thanksgiving Menu: Sports Are a Social Superconductor Bringing All Kinds of People Together," *New York Post*, November 22, 2022. https://nypost.com.
53. Quoted in Bobby Burack, "New Book Says Being a Sports Fan Improves Mental Health," Outkick, December 5, 2022. www.outkick.com.
54. Quoted in Ben Valenta and David Sikorjak, "The Perks of Being a Sports Fan: Cheering On a Team Has Benefits Beyond Game Day," Salon, November 12, 2022. www.salon.com.
55. Quoted in Valenta and Sikorjak, "The Perks of Being a Sports Fan."
56. Hari Dandapani, "Esports Epics," *Brown Daily Herald*, March 2, 2023. www.browndailyherald.com.
57. Quoted in Steve Harman, "91-Year-Old High School Sports Superfan Hasn't Missed a Game in Decades—Not Even After He Was Hit by Lightning," CBS Evening News, September 30, 2022. www.cbsnews.com.
58. Mike Schuster, "Mike Schuster's SuperFan Page," Tripod, 2022. https://members.tripod.com.
59. Dandapani, "Esports Epics."
60. George Dohrmann, *Superfans*. New York: Ballantine, 2018, p. xiii.

Books

Tanya Cook and Kaela Joseph, *Fandom Acts of Kindness*. Dallas: Smart Pop, 2023.

Leanne Currie-McGhee, *Anime and Manga Fandom*. San Diego: ReferencePoint, 2022.

Sheena C. Howard, *Why Wakanda Matters*. Dallas: Smart Pop, 2021.

Robb Pearlman and Jordan Hoffman, *The "Star Trek" Book of Friendship*. Dallas: Smart Pop, 2022.

Kaitlyn Tiffany, *Everything I Need I Get from You: How Fangirls Created the Internet as We Know It*. New York: MCD x FSG Originals, 2022.

Becca Wright, *BTS: Top of K-Pop: The Ultimate Fan Guide*. London: Buster, 2023.

Internet Articles

Joe Coscarelli, "How Pop Music Fandom Became Sports, Politics, Religion, and All-Out War," *New York Times*, December 25, 2020. www.nytimes.com.

Claire Murphy, "How Superfans of Harry Styles, Taylor Swift, Billie Eilish & More Are Changing Artist Merchandising with Consumable Fan Art," Recording Academy Grammy Awards, June 1, 2022. www.grammy.com.

Aja Romano, "Fandom Went Mainstream in the 2010s—for Better and Worse," Vox, December 30, 2019. www.vox.com.

Kaitlyn Tiffany, "How Deadheads and Directioners Made the Internet What It Is Today," Pitchfork, June 7, 2022. https://pitchfork.com.

Andrea Towers, "Cosplay and Conventions; How Being a Fan Helped Me Rediscover Myself," Popverse, September 21, 2022. www.thepopverse.com.

Ben Valenta and David Sikorjak, "The Perks of Being a Sports Fan: Cheering On a Team Has Benefits Beyond Game Day," Salon, November 12, 2022. www.salon.com.

Websites

Archive of Our Own

https://archiveofourown.org

This fan-created and -run website hosts an archive of more than 10 million works of fan fiction based on books, celebrities, bands, video games, anime, movies and television shows, and more. Users can upload stories and interact with others in fan communities.

Comic Book Resources

www.cbr.com

This fan-favorite website has tens of thousands of articles on manga, anime, American comics, cartoons, and games as well as reviews, lists, forums, and news.

Fandom

www.fandom.com

Fandom has more than 300 million monthly visitors and lists over 250,000 fan-powered wikis that hold 40 million pages of fandom content covering entertainment, gaming, and sports.

Popverse

www.thepopverse.com

Popverse is dedicated to fans who celebrate movies, television, and comics with news, articles, and other features covering Marvel, *Star Wars*, Batman, *Star Trek*, and anime and manga.

Twitch

www.twitch.tv

Twitch is an interactive live-streaming service for gaming, entertainment, sports, music, and more.

INDEX